The subject matter and vocabulary have been selected with expert assistance, and the brief and simple text is printed in large, clear type.

Children's questions are anticipated and facts presented in a logical sequence. Where possible, the books show what happened in the past and what is relevant today.

Special artwork has been commissioned to set a standard rarely seen in books for this reading age and at this price.

Full-colour illustrations are on all 48 pages to give maximum impact and provide the extra enrichment that is the aim of all Ladybird Leaders.

See back of book for index.

A Ladybird Leader

living things

written by Romola Showell

illustrated by David Palmer and Harry Wingfield

Ladybird Books Ltd Loughborough

You are alive.
You know that you are alive
because you move
and breathe, and feed
and grow.

But how do you know that the limpet,
seaweed and dandelion are alive?
Do they breathe and grow?
Can you see them move?
When you have read this book
you should know the answers.

Limpet

Seaweed

Dandelion

This is alive.

It is a very small animal called an Amoeba.

It lives in fresh water.

It is made up of one single unit called a cell.

These are very big living things.
They are made of millions of cells.
You are a living animal,
so you are made of cells too.

Plants are alive.

Most of them do not move very much
but they grow and feed.

They have to breathe, as well.

All living things must
feed and breathe.

Animals are alive.
Most of them move about,
and they grow and feed.
They have young ones.
All living things reproduce —
this means they lay eggs
or have young, such as the foal.

'Never-alive' things

Some things have never lived at all.
The objects in this picture
are all made of metals.
Metals have never been alive.
Most rocks, are 'never-alive' things.

Some things are dead.
They have once been alive.
This chair is made of wood.
The wood was once part
of a living tree.

You may not think you are very much like a goldfish or a horse.
And you don't eat the same things as a sparrow.

But you all breathe and feed.

You all had to have a mother and a father.

You cannot fly like a butterfly but you can move about.

Growth

These are baby animals.

They will all grow.

They will grow to the normal size for each animal.

They grow because their cells increase in number.

Plants grow too.
This is an acorn.
If it is planted it will grow into
an oak tree.

Even tiny seeds, such as willow-herb
will grow into plants.

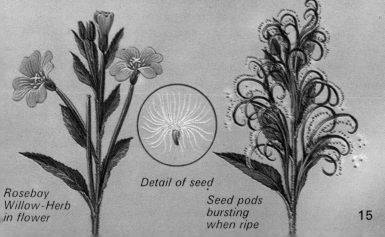

Rosebay
Willow-Herb
in flower

Detail of seed

Seed pods
bursting
when ripe

15

There is air all around you.
You cannot see it,
but without it you would die.
You need the oxygen in the air
to keep you alive.

Nearly all living things need oxygen.
Many of them get their oxygen
from the air.
Even when animals are sleeping
they breathe and take in oxygen.

The need for oxygen

Plants need oxygen to stay alive.

A plant seed may look dry and dead
but if it has oxygen it can stay alive
often for several years.

It will not grow until it gets water, too.

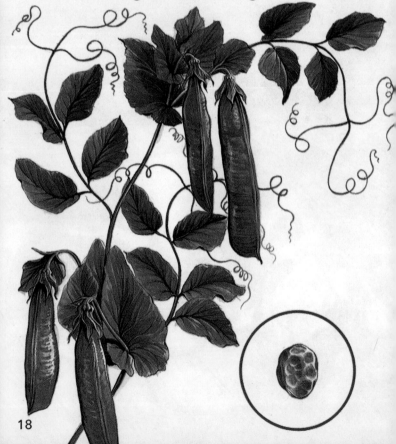

Some plants and animals live in water.
They have to get their oxygen
from the water.
A fish has gills
to help it get oxygen from the water.

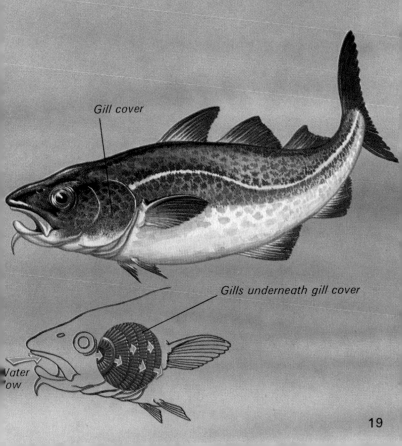

Gill cover

Gills underneath gill cover

Water
flow

How living things move

Living things move in different ways.
Some crawl. Some fly.

Some swim
and some are
jet-propelled.

Octopus

Many of them move about
using their legs.

The mammals and reptiles use their
four legs and some of them
move very fast indeed.

Cheetahs, like the one shown here,
can run at nearly 70 miles (113 km) an hour

How living things move

Some have many legs,
like the centipede.

And some, the insects,
have six legs.

*Cockchafer
Beetle*

Spiders have eight legs,
but all these animals move about.

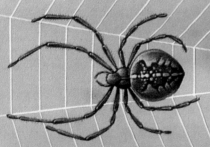

Garden Spider

They need to move
so that they can find their food.

Very few plants can move
from one place to another,
but they do move.

They move their leaves
so that they are in the light.

23

Food for living things

All living things need food,
but they do not need all the
same things.

Animals that live mainly on flesh
are called carnivores.

Those that live on plants
are called herbivores.

Some very large animals live on plants,

and so do some very small ones.

How plants feed

Plants feed,
but they have to make their food
from some very simple things.

They build up their food
from carbon dioxide
(a gas which is in the air)
and from water.

Carbon dioxide

Water and
mineral salts

To make their food
they need the energy in sunlight.
With sunlight the green leaves
make food from the carbon dioxide,
water and mineral salts,
which are dissolved in the water
they get from the soil.

Food

Food chains

All animals–even if they are flesh eaters –depend on plants for food.

Plankton

Small crustaceans

Wheat seeds

Field mice

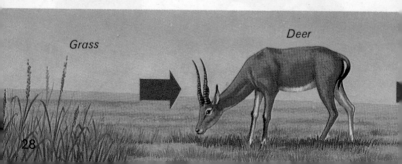

Grass

Deer

These are called 'food chains'.
Each stage is a 'link' in a 'chain'.

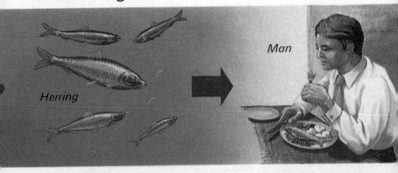

Herring → Man

→ Barn Owl

Lion

Animals that lay eggs

These are baby blackbirds.
The hen blackbird laid the eggs
and they hatched into these babies.

All living things reproduce.
This means they have young ones.

Birds are not the only animals
to lay eggs.
All these lay eggs.
The baby animals hatch from the eggs.

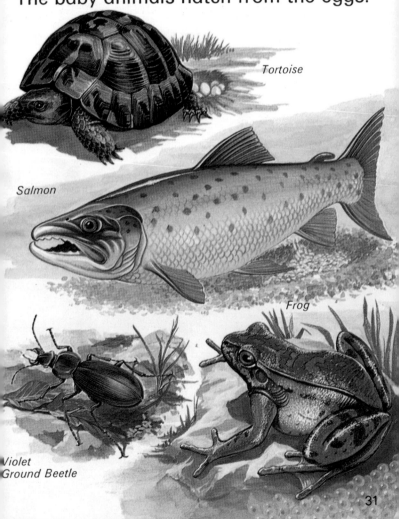

Tortoise

Salmon

Frog

Violet
Ground Beetle

31

Mammals are animals where babies grow inside the mother animal until they are ready to be born.

After they are born the mother feeds them with milk from her body.

Most babies look more or less
like their parents.
But do you know what this will
grow into?

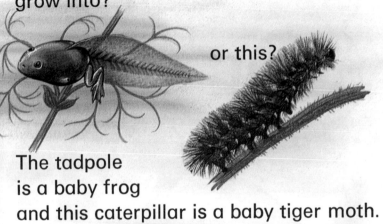

or this?

The tadpole
is a baby frog
and this caterpillar is a baby tiger moth.

Tiger Moth

Plants that have seeds

Plants have seeds.
The seeds will grow into new plants.

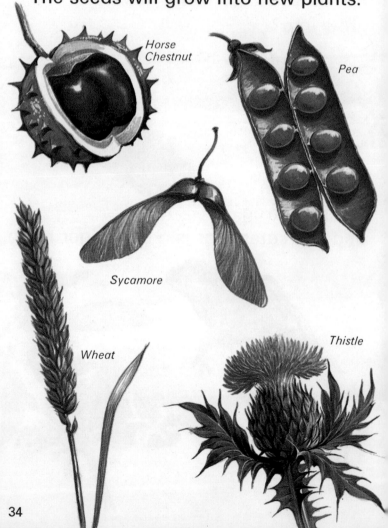

Horse Chestnut

Pea

Sycamore

Wheat

Thistle

New plants from bulbs and roots

It is possible to grow new plants
without seeds.

This is a tulip bulb.
It will grow into a plant.

This is couch grass.
It sends out long underground stems,
and new roots and leaves grow from
these stems to start new plants.

There are millions of kinds of
living things on earth.
You will never be able to see them all.
Some are very common,
but some are very rare.

Some of the animals which once lived
are now extinct.

Extinct means that there are
no more of them left alive.

Tyrannosaurus

These animals have bones.
They all have a skeleton
made of bones.

The skeleton supports the body,
the skull protects the brain,
and the ribs protect the lungs.

Mouse

Minnow

Toad

Robin

This is the skeleton of a cat.
Where the bones meet
you can see the joints.
If there were no joints
the animal could not move.

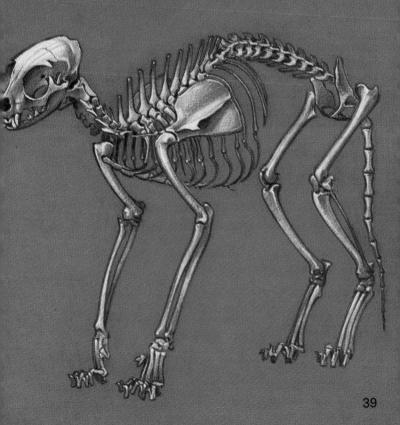

Skeletons and shells

Some animals such as crabs, have hard outer shells.

Crab

Shrimp

Some have neither bones nor shells, and are soft.

Sea anemone

Jellyfish

You are a mammal
so you have bones.

Birds, fish, reptiles,
and amphibians also have bones.

41

Insects

There are more kinds of insects
than any other animals in the world.
More than three quarters
of all living animals are insects.

Garden tiger moth

Lacewing

Wasp

Common
grasshopper

Ladybird

Stag Beetle

Ladybird

Devil's
coach
horse

Earwig

Migratory locust
(a rare visitor)

Dragonfly

Most insects go through several stages in their lives.

This is the life story of a butterfly.

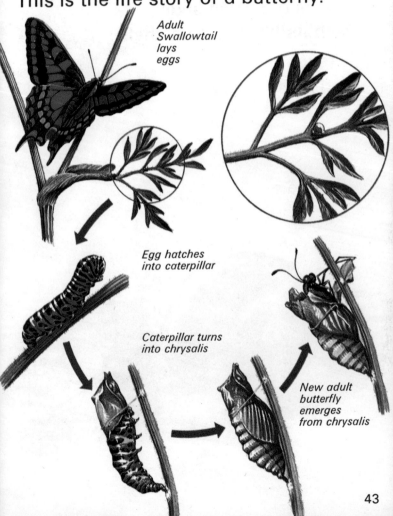

Adult Swallowtail lays eggs

Egg hatches into caterpillar

Caterpillar turns into chrysalis

New adult butterfly emerges from chrysalis

There are many other small animals
that you know.
This is a garden snail
with its hard, brown shell.
It feeds on leaves
and lays its eggs in the soil.

These are spiders.
They have just hatched
from their mother's eggs.

They are very small
but they grow quickly.

They feed on flies and other insects.

The Coast redwood
can grow to more than
367 feet (112 m) tall
longer than
a professional size
football pitch

This plant is the tallest in the world,
and is called a Coast redwood.

Like all living things it breathes, feeds,
grows and reproduces.

This little plant floats
on the top of ponds.
It is called duckweed.
It, too, breathes, feeds, grows
and reproduces.

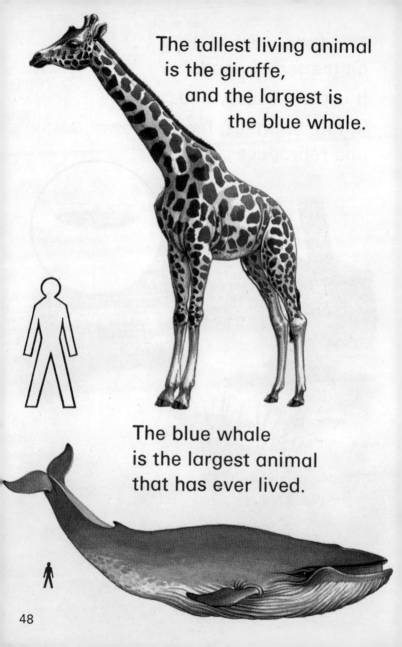

The tallest living animal
is the giraffe,
and the largest is
the blue whale.

The blue whale
is the largest animal
that has ever lived.

Many insects and most birds can fly,
but the only flying mammals
are the bats.

If you have read all this book you know quite a lot about living things. You know that there are plants and animals and you know that they breathe, feed, grow, move and reproduce.

Look around you.

Look at all the living things that you can see every day.

Remember that all animals and plants are living.

Try to find out more about them.

INDEX

	page
Acorn	15
Amoeba	6
Bats	49
Beetle	
cockchafer	22
stag	42
violet ground	31
Blackbirds	30
Bones	38, 39
Bulbs	35
Butterfly	13
swallowtail	43
Calf	32
Carbon dioxide	26
Cat, skeleton	39
Caterpillar	33, 43
Centipede	22
Cheetah	21
Chrysalis	43
Clover	25, 26
Coast redwood	46
Couch grass	35
Cow	32
Crab	40
Crustacea	28
Dandelion	5
Deer	28
Devil's coach horse	42
Dog	17, 36

	page
Dragonfly	42
Duckling	14
Duckweed	47
Earwig	42
Eggs	30
beetle	31
butterfly	43
frog	31, 33
salmon	31
spider	45
tortoise	31
Elephant	25
Fish	19
Foal	9
Food chains	28, 29
Food	24
for animals	24, 25
for insects	45
for plants	26, 27
for small animals	44
Frog	31, 33
Gills	19
Giraffe	48
Goldfish	13
Grasshopper	42
Growth	14
Herring	29
Horse	9, 12
Horse chestnut	34